WE SKATE HARDCORE

WE SKATE HARDCORE
VINCENT CIANNI

PHOTOGRAPHS FROM BROOKLYN'S SOUTHSIDE

PUBLISHED BY NEW YORK UNIVERSITY PRESS

NEW YORK AND LONDON

AND LYNDHURST BOOKS OF THE
CENTER FOR DOCUMENTARY STUDIES AT DUKE UNIVERSITY

DURHAM, NORTH CAROLINA

Grand Street from my window

"I started skating because I simply liked it. . . .
This possibility drives so many kids nowadays.
In this possibility the egos, desires for acceptance,
praise, and self-affirmation kick around happily.
You start to dream about what you can 'become.'"
—Nick Riggle, *Daily Bread* magazine

In 1992 I moved to a loft in the Greenpoint section of Brooklyn, New York. That year, on my way home from work, I often passed by the Southside in Williamsburg to stop at Hector's tacqueria on Bedford Avenue near Grand Street. I was enamored by the vitality, sounds, and smells of the streets in the Latino neighborhood. By November 1993 I had found a place to live and work just around the corner from Hector's. I hired Beto, whose mother owned the video store across the street, and his friend Angel to help me carry furniture up to my second-floor loft in a former warehouse building. For the first year I concentrated on fixing up the raw space. Hector's, the bakery, and the corner bodega on the other end of the block became central to my daily life and the focus of my attempts to speak more Spanish.

During a warm break in the weather in the fall of 1994 I began going to McCarren Park, drawn by the neighborhood activities and games played on the park's soccer and baseball fields, on its track and handball courts. The park is the largest in the neighborhood, some three blocks of open green space bustling with energy. Young men smash handballs against cement walls, kick soccer balls with the grace of dancers and strength of weightlifters, and hit and catch baseballs with intense determination, wearing uniforms of their own design. Families gather on weekends to picnic and barbecue, particularly on holidays and Puerto Rican day celebrations. Shrieks and yells for outstanding plays or defeated attempts as well as salsa music permeate the air, mixing with the smell of cuchifrito or rice and beans. I began making portraits of teenagers playing ball in McCarren and the other parks, in schoolyards, and on the streets and sidewalks of the Southside.

The Southside's boundaries create a neighborhood of seven square blocks with distinct borders—the East River to the west, the Brooklyn-Queens Expressway (BQE) to the east, and Metropolitan Avenue and Broadway to the north and south, respectively. Built by Robert Moses in 1954, the BQE effectively cut the neighborhood in two. The Williamsburg Bridge, spanning the East River, connects the Southside to Manhattan's Lower East Side. During the 1990s, the Bridge was, like the neighborhoods around it, gritty and often dangerous, until renovations were completed in 2002. Over the years Williamsburg's waterfront has decayed, leaving behind underutilized and abandoned industrial buildings that were once the sources of the neighborhood's wealth and culture.

Inside the Southside, life unfolds in an ever-changing but always familiar urban landscape. A predominately Hispanic neighborhood, it is a somewhat isolated environment, protected by its well-defined geographic and cultural boundaries. Yet because of its easy accessibility to Manhattan, the Southside has the same social ills and problems of the greater city surrounding it. In this environment of violence, drugs, and urban blight, there are also strong social, religious, and family structures, and the kids who grow up here share a peculiar blend of street smarts and innocence influenced in equal part by popular culture and ethnic identity.

View from Uly's roof, South 5th Street

My whole life IVE LIVED in the same Apartment, In the same Hispanic Populated area for 21 years. I Live with my mother Because my father Passed away this summer so SHE Has Been Really Depressed Lately, And I love her Dearly. SHE'S ALWAYS BEEN THERE FOR ME IN GOOD + BAD SITUATIONS. TO EVERYONE ELSE LIVING IN NEW YORK IS A WONDERFUL EXPERIENCE. BUT ITS GOTTEN A LITTLE BORING TO ME AT TIMES. SOMETIMES I WISH I WERE AWAY FROM EVERYTHING, BUT NO MATTER WHAT I ALWAYS THINK ABOUT MY HOMETOWN. ITS IRONIC HOW I

HATE MY
BUT YET IF I
ALWAYS WANT
BACK HOME.
HOME AND WILL
I'M SURE
IF I MOVE
WILL MISS IT
WONT BOTHER
COME BACK
THE ONLY
WILL AFFECT
FRIENDS
BEHIND.
MY LIFE IS
OF THE TIME
or DOING ODD
MONEY FOR THE
JAN 12 I START
WORKING FOR
SOMETHING I
AND IT WILL
I DO SOME
WEEKENDS
IN CLUBS

NIECHBORHOOD
LEAVE IT I
TO COME
FOR ME ITO
ALWAYS BE.
THOUGH THAT
AWAY I
BUT IT
ME IF I
or NOT
THING THAT
ME IS THE
I LEFT
SIMPLE, most
I'M SKATING
JOBS TO MAKE
WEEKEND, ON
A NEW JOB
PARKS, CLEANING
FIND INTEREST'N,
HELP PAY BILLS
JOBS ON THE
PLAYING MUSIC
e PARTYS. ITS A

GOOD WAY TO MAKE A QUICK 600 A WEEK. THE REASON I SKATE IS BECAUSE THE FEELING I GET. A RUSH, FREEDOM FROM OTHERS AND IT KEEPS STRESS FROM MY MIND. USUALLY WHEN I'M REALLY mad I go out + SKATE, I GET HURT REALLY BAD, BUT I DONT care my stress is RELIEVED. I ALSO ENJOY HANGING OUT WITH MY FRIENDS, WE ALL USUALLY SIT TOGETHER AND JOKE ABOUT EACH OTHER. ITS ALWAYS ULI THAT CRACKS THE JOKES.

Richie, P.S. 84

I met Anthony at McCarren Park playing handball. After a few games, I asked if I could make a portrait of him. He was nineteen years old with tattoos on his arms and a scar down the center of his stomach from an operation to repair abdominal damage sustained in a knife fight. That day, I also made some images of kids playing baseball. I soon began photographing other teenagers in the neighborhood. These young men expressed their masculinity in the ways they chose to dress and ornament their bodies. Their faces, clothing, and postures communicated a pride that mixed curiosity with self-assurance, vulnerability with arrogance. Their assertion of masculinity seemed a disguise for their naiveté and innocence. A year or two later I started photographing the Southside's young women. They were not as accessible as the adolescent boys because they were more protected and not given as much freedom to hang out in the streets.

Anthony, McCarren Park

Uly, P.S. 84

This is me. Why Doing a negative mitsue.
A trik meany people have tryied todo But not Like one.
I enipy to skate Because it's fun and
I spend mad time with my boy Rich.
I have made fun with him Because we could
relate to one onther   Also he uneereges me
to do positive thing's Like going back to school.

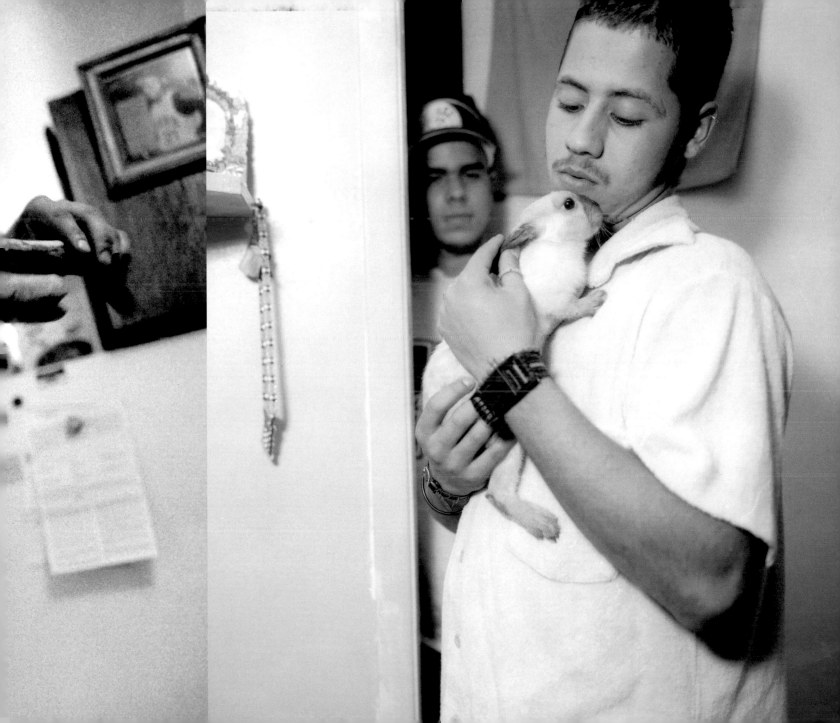

This is me and my girl Dee. Dee is verry Unique cause of the person she is.
Dee made a baby girl at the age of 16 y old. She raised her baby girl and finised high shool.
And also did some college. She's a hard worker and also smart I guess that makes her a

The strage women you see here with me.
Dee helps keep my life in Balance. She helps me accomplesh my goals,
and reminds me to presious the thing I have, and what I Have
Dar.

This is me and my Dad Hanging Out, This is His room
in awer House.   We like to talk and
smoke weed, or pot if you may.   My family
is same what upsite of the relationship We Have.
But I realy dont give a fuck, cuzlse where Happy
and there Not My Dad is my Best friend and farther.
We fight But never forget What We Have.

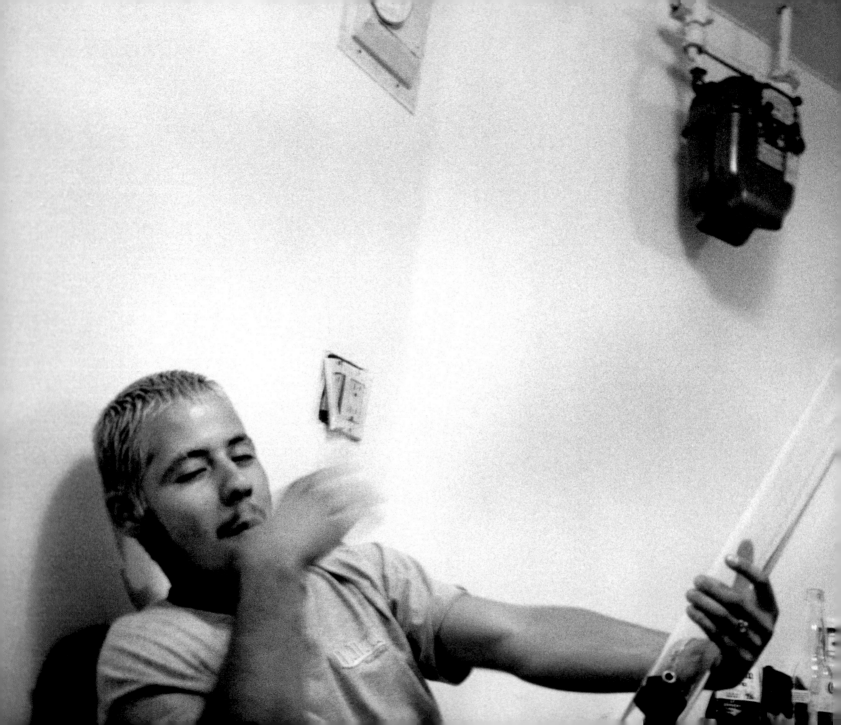

From Nelson: Here Nelson is throwing a stick at the
light post trying to break the bulb!!

I was photographing a group of young in-line skaters on the street and in a vacant lot on the East River. They had constructed an impressive set of ramps, pipes, and slides on which they practiced every day. Some weeks later I returned, and they were gone. A developer had purchased the land and fenced it in to prevent the skaters from using his property. A few months later I saw Anthony, who had helped build the skate park. He was on his way to a tattoo parlor; I went with him. When I mentioned that I hadn't seen the skaters, he said they were now at Marcy Avenue under the BQE and he would take me there that afternoon. On the way, Anthony noticed Giselle, five years his junior, walking with her friend Vivien. He stopped to ask her for a date, smoothly maneuvering her toward a fence. Instinctively, I photographed them while Vivien waited impatiently in the background; I immediately recognized how the camera's spontaneity and capacity to tell stories intimately would change how I photographed.

The skaters' new park under the elevated highway followed the fate of the one by the East River when neighbors on the "other side" of Williamsburg complained to the city. Sanitation trucks came, and workers tore down and carted off the ramps and slides. The skaters were not defeated; skating was their only way to escape from drugs and the street. They went from vacant lots to abandoned buildings constructing skate parks from scrap material. Their parks existed only until vandals destroyed them or sanitation trucks disposed of the ramps and pipes, or property owners evicted them from their run-down warehouses. I followed them to the BQE, to P.S. 84, and then to an abandoned building on the East River. They were making their own photographs and videotapes "to enhance their technique," and all the while they were organizing local in-line skating, skateboarding, and BMX competitions, and drawing up plans for a skate park to present to the community board.

Anthony hitting on Giselle

Under the Brooklyn-Queens Expressway

RICHIE: We decided to build some ramps under the BQE [Brooklyn-Queens Expressway]. What we did is we got a group of rollerbladers together, and we just went on building these ramps. It was illegal because we had it in an area that was for parking, but nobody was using it. So we figured, "Let's build it there," and we did it. We started with some small ramps; then other friends came over and helped build better ramps; the biggest one was about four feet.

I always say this because it was true for me—it wasn't a place to skate but a place for everybody to meet other people. I met so many people there that I didn't know before. That was my experience.

That's why I felt like I had to push out to continue this. We seen that this park brought together so many people, you know. Everybody wasn't distant. Everybody was together. Whenever anybody met each other, they introduced themselves, and that's what made me realize that we have to continue this and start with our organization, which we're starting now, and our park, which will be done maybe in a year. Even though it's a long time. . . . Hey, something is something, and I will be continuing with this until, I guess . . . just forever—because it's not just about me skating it— it's about everybody else skating it.

MECCA: As a matter of fact, I was with them when they were building it. I was sort of there from the beginning. We had started and we had small ramps. Some ramps were already built. If you go there now—the park area we had—there's about two or three cars there. And it was like a good space because it was like shelter. It was a place for kids to be without getting in trouble because we didn't have to go trash city steps and rails; we didn't have to worry about the cops coming and kicking us out.

We had a couple of incidents where the police, they came over, but you know they didn't have a problem with us, being that we were out of the way. We weren't back and forth; it was one set area where everybody could come and meet. And it was good for the sport.

We had a party, and a lot of people came. We had a band there. We didn't really stay out late; they made sure that we closed at 10:30. They turned the ramp over, made sure, you know, that nobody was skating so that we wouldn't cause trouble. To me, I think it was a good idea. It was good for the kids because you know it kept them out of trouble—a place to go . . . so that they had friends, and when the kids had nobody else [at home] they came over and had family support. It gave me this warm, cozy feeling.

RICHIE: That's all right. The next one we do will be in Eagle Park. Opens at ten, closes at eight. No ifs, ands, or buts about it, because we're going to enforce the law. We're talkin' about helmets, wrist guards, elbow pads, knee pads; we're talkin' about the works for it to be a safety place . . . either that or just don't skate here.

In a way I was kind of glad they left it there that long—I was surprised. But I was mad the way they did it. They should of notified us first . . . so we would have had time to put it someplace else.

We had two professionally built ramps, and both of them were trashed. It cost a lot of money. I myself put out over $300 to build that park.

MICHELLE: The park was built by the skaters—no help from anybody. The materials used came from the skaters. We needed nails, the skaters put up the money, everything. Unfortunately, we put it in an area where we weren't wanted, I guess.

RICHIE: It was a race thing.

MICHELLE: Every time that kids—Latinos, blacks, whatever—try, you know, to do some good. . . . We wanted to build a park, we built it. That's what we like, we like skating. We wanted to have a place where we could skate. Every time we want to do something good, it seems that something comes and just stomps us on down and does not want us to get better, does not want us to, you know, overcome stereotypes that we're lazy, that all we do is shoot people and kill and rob.

We finally wanted to do something good. It's not a white, Latino, black thing. It's not that . . . we had so many races, people from everywhere. People would come with their families and just stay watching us and everything. It was great. And we do not know why . . . they just did not leave it there.

Instead they just decided one day, when we weren't there, to come without notice. They didn't let us take our ramps. They didn't let us take the rails, nothing. Just tear everything down and take it away. Some of the people were like, "Oh, it's great there." The people from around there, you know, they were like, "Nah! We don't want this. These aren't doing any good." They were saying that we were jumping over cars. We went to a [community] board meeting and this lady—I was speaking—and she tells me, "I saw you jumping over cars." I'm like, "Whoa! If I could jump over a car, it would be great!" But I can't jump over a car. There was nobody jumping over cars.

Maybe it was the noise or something. We couldn't stay there late. So we decided, all right let's make some moves. We had the place clean. I mean we bought the brooms, everything.

MECCA: We had a sweeping crew.

MICHELLE: We had a time that everybody had to leave. At first it was, like, 11:00 or something, and then it was 10:00. Everybody just had to leave. And you know it was working out, and all of a sudden our park was gone one day. We just all came and—[it] was like, "Hey! Where's the BQE? It's gone! Sanitation took it away."

RICHIE: We had one [community board meeting] before; we had one after; and we're having some now. [The neighbors] complained about noise. They even one day tried to put it upon us that we were stealing cars, because a friend of mine got his car stolen right around the corner from where we were at. They were saying, "Those damn rollerbladers, whatever, whatever . . . skateboarders." That was something that surprised [me] because it was a late-night thing, and we weren't even in the park at that time.

Michelle made a speech in the community board, and they loved it! They loved it! Because they like to see young people do this.

They gave us a guy to work with. He had about six projects to do; he had to finish them by a certain date, one of them was ours, and he didn't even want to put any effort into it. So I took it upon myself to do this by myself to say, "The hell with it. Let me try to do this by myself." And without his help, you know, I got together everybody and just started all over again by November. We've been working on it for about six months.

MICHELLE: They gave us some offers. They were coming up to us and they were like, "Oh! Here's my card . . . get in touch with us." So like, when we actually did get in touch . . .

RICHIE: The brush-off!

MICHELLE: It was like, "Oh, you! Oh, the kids I gave the cards to! Oh, OK," and it's like they were only doing it for the time being after we gave the speech. But then, when it came to actually doing action about it, they were just putting us off. And Richie, he really took it into his own hands. He was like, "Forget this!" He got in touch with somebody that could really help us. And now they're telling us, "Oh . . . we're going to give you this park."

It's a big mess! It's going to take time, a lot of time.

RICHIE: Before May 17th, we have to do a budget plan; we have to do a couple of more meetings; we have to do a couple of more proposals. And before May 17th, we have to put in a—what is it they call it—just to say that we're going to occupy that space for the park and that we have to find out how much money it's going to be, which is going to be a lot, maybe. I mean, I don't know how much, but it's going to be a lot of money because these parks usually take a lot of money. And we're just going to deal with that park. . . . We wanted McCarren pool. If we can fight for it, it would be even better because that would probably be the biggest park in the East Coast, maybe even in the world, because it's such a big area. So, you know, we're fighting for it, but we have a park put up already.

THE AFTERMATH:

This picture was taken after the City tore o
under nieth the BQE expressway. Then we moved
North 11th street.

I think that this spot was the place for
It was easy to get to. Convenient for us, it brun
local stores.

skate Park down

ur site to

great Park

usiness to the

Uly videotaping at the BQE

EDDIE: We all spent days and days building these big huge ramps that were so sweet—
they were throwin' so high in the air—all of us, everybody. We had it for the whole summer, right?
We had it for a little more than the whole summer. And there was on the block right where
we were at—we were underneath the BQE—right across the street there was a block, and on that
block there's mostly elderly people, and they did not want us there. We didn't know whether it was
racist or whatever, but we know that they just didn't want us there for some reason. They used
to always complain, and one of them had the sanitation department come and destroy everything in
the middle of the night. And we know that it wasn't sanitation on their own because sanitation
used to come themselves, and they used to clean up for us. . . . We had garbage cans. That place
was never dirty. Every time the people would eat stuff or drink stuff, we always had garbage
cans and sanitation used to come and take our garbage bags.

MIKE R.: [At P.S. 84] we got a handrail goin' down the steps; they broke it in three pieces.

EDDIE: I think it was somebody from over here; somebody from this side. In the night we hang
out here until about 10:00, something like that. And some people come here to hang out later than
us, and they make a lot of noise. Sometimes we get blamed for it. I think they broke our rails,
so we wouldn't hang here in the night.

EDDIE: This is what's left of a rail. [Ralph had carried over a piece of the rail.] It was a straight,
flat-ground rail. It was about twenty-feet long. Some asshole come and destroyed it, and when we
find out who it is, they're going to be just like this rail. If they're lucky, they'll be in three pieces.

EDDIE: We're here at 84. We're everyday skaters here—just doin' our thing.

MIKE R.: We skate hardcore.

EDDIE: Yeah, we do aggressive skating, none of this recreational stuff.

MIKE R.: Skating is fun.

EDDIE: You can get hurt. It gives you a rush.

MIKE R.: Like when you jump on a handrail, it feels so good. And doin' ramps, like, catchin' the air. It's like a rush.

EDDIE: There's a lot of different companies out there now. You got a lot of different skate companies, clothes companies. . . . If you're good enough, and if you have the connections, you can get into these companies and start getting all types of free stuff, and it's really cool. You don't have to pay for anything any more. It's either you work, you ask your parents, or you better hope you're sponsored, or you have sponsored friends.

MIKE R.: And that's why we videotape ourselves. So we can send it out to a sponsor.

EDDIE: We like to watch ourselves skate. Obviously you can't see yourself when you're skating. Everyone else can see you, but you can't see yourself. Sometimes it's good to record yourself, so you can see what you could do to improve, or [see] what you like, what you're more comfortable with, how your style looks. It's all about style in this game. That's what this is—it's really a game. It's a sport, but it's also a game because it's so fun.

EMILIO: Why did I start? To kill time, really. It was fun. I saw it was dangerous and everything. I just wanted to kill time.

POPO: Mucho fun, you know!

Ricky at my place

Monica and Eddie, P.S. 84

HAVE YOU SEEN THIS CHILD, IF ~~WE~~ YOU ~~WE~~ HAVE SEEN THIS CHILD HE GOES →

BY THE NAME OF JOSEPH MEDINA, LAST SEEN ON T.C. TELEPHONE COMP.
WEARING A POLO SPORT SWEATER AND STUDA BAKER STRETCH JEANS
IF YOU SEE HIM CALL !!!!!!!!!!!!!!!5   THANK YOU
, RICHIE RICH.

Emilio get demented when he sets on his skates. He jumps the fars, and sickes & gaps. If it wasn't for him and all my skating friends lme wouldn't be skating right now. By Dean Rodriguez

prObe

In autumn 1996 I was photographing a group of girls on South 2nd Street when five men from a nearby auto body shop approached and confronted me about why I was photographing the girls. I put my camera down on the sidewalk and explained that I lived in the neighborhood and was making portraits of teenagers as part of documenting the community. They were suspicious of my intentions and warned me to stop photographing the girls and leave the block. People gathered around; I agreed not to take photographs of the girls but insisted on staying there with my camera. The men went back to the shop; I picked up my camera and began taking pictures of other kids. A few days later I went to the auto body shop and showed the owner, the father of one of the girls, contact prints of the portraits I had been making. After he finished looking at them, he invited me to a block party that coming weekend after the Puerto Rican Day parade. We became fast friends.

I continued taking pictures in the neighborhood, frequenting social clubs and places of worship. I was invited to parties and cultural and religious celebrations in the homes of people I knew. I remember the sounds of kids playing in the street; of music reverberating from car stereos and apartment windows, bodies moving, voices singing; of dominoes slapping down on tables set up on the sidewalks in front of bodegas; of babies crying in the arms of young mothers, bright colors stretched across bronzed bodies. Ads in Spanish were plastered layer upon layer in the windows and on the walls of neighborhood shops. I began spending time in Maria's social club drinking a beer or playing pool on summer afternoons, or I would squeeze into a small restaurant on South 2nd Street Saturday nights to dance merengue. Sometimes I simply passed the time standing in front of Ernie's house with his family.

Sugeiry touching Scarface with a knife

Stephen and Jamie installing a radio

Stephen and Ricky, Grand Street

Mike R., P.S. 84

It's like, it's like, all you see is kids hanging out everywhere here smokin'—kids selling
drugs all around this area. But me, I don't want to be one of them. I want to be a skater.
I want to be a pro skater and make, um, my own films. That's what I want.

Mike R. skating down Stuyvesant rail, lower Manhattan

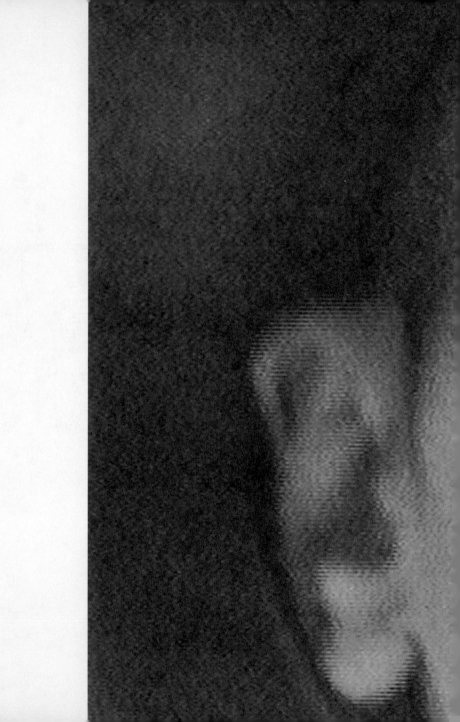

Jesus, Mullaly Skate Park, The Bronx

MIKE R.: We don't skate everyday.

EDDIE: Yes we do, stop lying. We skate everyday.

POPO: He don't skate everyday. *We* skate everyday.

MIKE R.: No, we skate everyday. But, I mean, we don't skate *here* everyday.

We go to Manhattan, Queens, Bronx . . . Peter Pan rails, everywhere.

EDDIE: Because it's boring here everyday. Can't stay in one spot.

POPO: And, like, then, we can learn new tricks. We go in a rail, and we see new people, new rails, new tricks, and we can learn from some other people.

Shorty jumping the stairs, Bedford Avenue

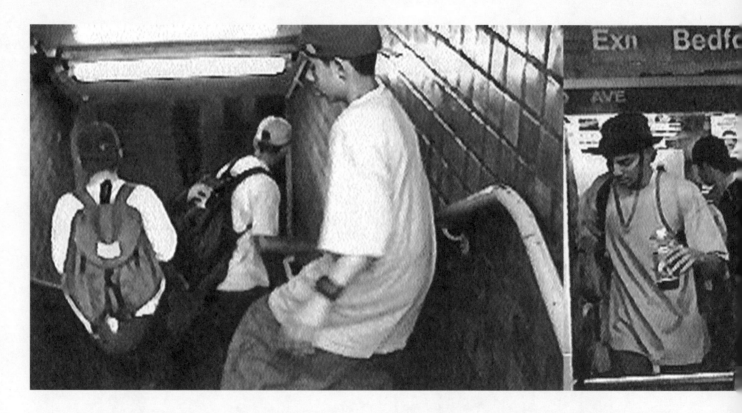

JESUS: We're going to Mullaly Skate Park in The Bronx, the part of The Bronx where the New York Yankees are, and that skate park is pretty old. All the ramps are like torn down and shit. So, it's going to be pretty fun . . . because they have, like, a mini. They have a huge launch about six-feet high and shit. So it's pretty bad. And they have a spine. The spine is about four feet off the ground. They got some nice transitions, I mean, you know what I'm saying—for what it is—it's a free park. The kids have to climb over the gate to get in, and during the summer they run the park, and they fix the park up, and you don't have to wear a helmet on certain days and shit. We're going on like a day when nobody [park officials] goes. It was closed down for a while because kids pulled their wrists and shit; they weren't wearing protective gear, and they were hurting themselves pretty bad.

RICHIE: It's an area that everybody goes to hang out. It's really cool. It's kind of like what we had [at the BQE], and it's only a little bit bigger. True, it's unsupervised, but it's also that we don't bother no one. And we like to go there to hang out because we don't have any other parks like this one. This is a park where we can practice anything that we want to without having anyone saying anything. It gives everybody a rush. If you know what you're doing, then you're doing all right, because if the ability is there, [the danger] doesn't affect you—because you know how to do the tricks, and you know how to do whatever you can.

VICTOR: It's like in the summertime there's a lot of spectators, and everything like that. Folks come around here, have fun. They end up having to fix the ramps all over again because during the wintertime bikers and bladers destroy [them] or vandals come around. . . . They'll just destroy it for no reason. But hey, I hope this time they [park officials] fixed it up, and it has better ramps. Usually this will be packed with so many skaters that bikers have to leave, or they just have to wait till we leave or vice versa. Same thing. Bikers may come here, rule it out, you know, but on a nice day like this, I think it should be pretty good. I hope so.

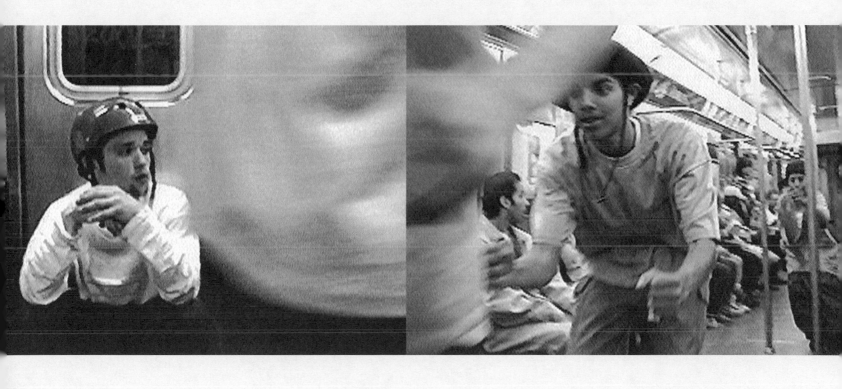

VICTOR: Rollerblading started out for me because as a young one around my neighborhood I was attracted to drugs and all of that stuff, you know, all the violence. Before I was rollerblading, I was smoking weed, doing things like hanging out with my friends. My cousin introduced me to it. You know, my first pair of rollerblades was some cheap recreational skates. And, you know, I got so into it that I just wanted to do it everyday, and then finally I got my skates. I had met a couple of friends, and then we got together; we made up a team. Then the team, that team, was called "Who's Next," and then I guess it died out because there was a lot of negative people in it. Like they were all smokin' weed and stuff. We didn't want that, you know. It was all a positive side. So now I've been rollerblading for about two years, you know, upgrading my level.

I started out smoking weed; I was at least twelve going on thirteen. I did it for about a year and a half, two years, close to two years. [When you rollerblade,] you get an adrenaline rush. It's your natural high. You know, you like pull a trick, a sick trick, and you stick to it, and that's what gets you hyped up. It keeps you high, and so you could just keep on going crazy and doing more certain tricks on it. That's what gets us going. The tricks is what gets us going, you know; it's completing that certain rail, that's what gets our high up, you just keep on going. That's what keeps me into skating—pulling a new trick, and doing it on a sick rail or a standard rail. And then I get to push my level up, and I just get to do it everyday, and once I get it, you know . . . we'll hang out, just chill.

Someday I would like to go professional; I wouldn't mind it. Skating isn't my life, you know, there's other things I want to do as in going to college and everything like that. But I wouldn't mind becoming professional and making money out of it, or whatever, and just skating for the fun of it. You know, that's what I do—I skate just to skate. I hang out with my friends, and I like to do that. That's what keeps me out of all that negative stuff in my neighborhood.

Your accomplishment is the important thing. Once you accomplish your goals and stuff, you set new goals and just keep on trying and trying and then when you feel that you've set all your goals, you just go onto a different sport, or you just keep on going until the sport just enhances. You know, right now rollerblading is enhancing very much. There's a lot of skaters out there; they do commercials, get inside movies. As I said, those are skaters that are very lucky. They set their goals in order to do that.

Victor on the subway

Mullaly Skate Park, The Bronx

The Factory, North 11th Street

This factory was the Hotspot for us skaters. Everyone ~~brough~~ brung inspiration to this underground skate park. It wasn't much compared to now but we had the best skate sessions here. Be it Bikes, Roller blades, Skate boards, even Snake boards we always tryed to make it a place of welcoming old and new people, whether you skated or not.

It is to bad that the city of New York never built Brooklyn a Skate park because all of the Community would have Benifited from this. I hope that every one in this Community

→ Im not Saying that they should Build a dam Skate park I'm Saying to listen to the youth in our Community. They are our future and we must listen to thier Plea's. But of course the Community is affraid of change thats why we'll stay stuck in the same Situation

Realizes how much of a heart break it was not to help us. We did everything for the Community to accept us — shows, clean-ups, volunteer work, and what did we get from this — false promises. Of course their is still a chance for the Community leaders to cotablish faith from the youth of the Community. ↗

Here we are at north 11th street enjoying some laughs.
Im glad that someone was here to record them times Because
I miss them. I feel like Im in this picture enjoying the laughs

This brings Back lots of memories for me because I look at
Picture and remember little things about them, for instance the st
Is holding, well ~~the~~ we had a contest on who can balance it on o
the rope behind them was used as a tarzan rope or to g
Fix patches for the rain.

als in this

hat the first guy (Uli)

on the longest.

o the roof to

ULY's HOUSE WAS LIKE a SECOND Home TO me. NOW THAT I LIVE in OHIO, And I don't have any Real Friends like I had in NEW YORK (EXEPT FOR Pammy) my life has been a little tough.
I Feel a little home sick but I know I will get over it. I like it here but there is nothing like N.Y.

ULY was my friend and Brother. What ever he needed I helped him get, what ever I needed he helped me get. We were a family. Uly, his dad, and I would hang out and enjoy many laughs with them. It's been so hard living these past month with out seeing them.

Juanito's sixteenth birthday, Uly's apartment

ULISIS HOUSE IS THE SPOT. HERE WE ARE ADMIRING THE ULTIMATE BONG HIT. AS YOU CAN SEE

EVERY ONE IS MESMORIZED, YOU CAN JUST HEAR THIS PICTURE.

LEFT to Right → Juanito, Richie, Dean, Joe, Rickey, Ralphy, Ulisis.

OHHH, AHHH, Feel the smoke ~~Rushing~~ Rushing down your lungs. THOSE were the DAYS.

In ... my nieghborhood each year ON THE DAY OF A FRIENDS BIRTHDAY WE GIVE HIM THE Ghetto Birthday PUNCHES. Some times it GETS SILLY, some times it GETS Rough, Sometimes People laugh sometimes PEOPLE CRY, For the most

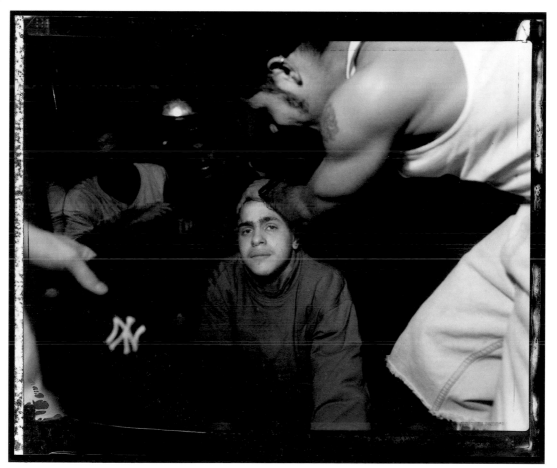

OF it, Its FUN. Juanito took it serious an started to tear. He's an alright kid but he punked out on us. THATS what happens when your in VLis House.

Richie on Broadway

In the 1970s, when the Rockefeller drug laws made it a felony for adults to possess and sell small amounts of drugs, the streets became tougher. The clockers—dealers on the street—were now in danger of being convicted and sentenced to stiff prison terms, and so minors inherited the job of selling drugs. These kids were now making money and were able to buy expensive sneakers, gold jewelry, and designer clothes, emblematic of their "gang status." When still-younger kids began attacking them with knives and stealing their prized possessions, the inexperienced, juvenile dealers acquired guns for protection. The cycle of violence shifted to the young. The young people of the Southside, as in other, similar neighborhoods, lived or died in it. By the 1990s, when I arrived, the landscape of the Southside was filled with altars and graffiti-covered walls, all made by friends and families commemorating young men who had been killed on the streets. Everywhere I saw reminders of lives lost to violence from dealing drugs, family arguments, jealousy, as well as to AIDS.

On Lorimer Street a mural of the cartoon characters Garfield and Odie pays tribute to Jeffrey, a twenty-five-year-old killed in a knife fight that started when he got angry that his girlfriend was flirting with another man. Jeffrey, like many young men in their teens and twenties, seemed to be irresistibly drawn to danger. The story of Jeffrey's death was in some way archetypal for the neighborhood.

Richie, Uly, Dean, Eddie, Mike R., and some of the other skaters would stop by my place to look at pictures I had made of them and to show me pictures and videos that they had made of themselves for sponsors and competitions. I began to interview and videotape them to document their lives more fully, and I asked them to write about their lives on my photographs. The bladers would come by and stay into the evening; I would make dinner while they wrote, made music with their hands, voices, whatever was laying around, and told stories of their recent accomplishments "pulling new tricks." They also talked about their efforts before the community board, which continually rejected their proposals for a skate park. They recognized their strengths and had their own dreams of success: to get sponsored by an in-line skate manufacturing company and turn pro; or to have a family, a house, a career, an office in Manhattan. They were aware of the obstacles that might prevent them from attaining the goals they desired; they were very honest and realistic about the neighborhood and their lives. Their words made perfect sense and enlightened me about my own life as I grew to understand their commitments, rites of passage, mistakes, and successes.

"It's a fucked-up day today, raining, over here in 84 Park in Southside, in Brooklyn, New York."—Mike R.

MIKE R.: I think we need skate parks around here, because we have no skate parks. I don't understand it. [There's] a lot of broken down lots where they could build big skate parks for the kids who skate.

EDDIE: Keep kids off the street.

MIKE R.: And they don't do it for them. . . . When you go to the West Coast, in Los Angeles, you see skate parks in every corner and shit.

EDDIE: A lot of the people that skate, especially out here in Brooklyn, a lot of us skate to stay out of trouble. I know I started skating to stay out of trouble because I was getting into a lot of trouble. Our neighborhood don't got shit. We skate where we can, and that's it. And if nobody likes it, that's too bad for them. Build us a park, and we'll stay out of your area.

RALPH: We used to have a park, and they tore it down; we used to have a rail, they tore it down.

MIKE R.: We used to have our own ramps.

RALPH: We have no choice.

EDDIE: When we had that BQE, no one was skating anywhere else but that park. We had rails, ramps, everything to keep everyone happy. Now all of a sudden, everything is torn down. If you didn't want us to skate elsewhere, you should have left us alone in the first place.

POPO: Why do I rollerblade? Because I like it.

EDDIE: It's like crack. Once you try it, you get hooked.

POPO: Yeah! I like being with all my homeboys, rollerblading around the area. People know us, and all that you know. [Shouts out in Spanish.]

RALPH: It's just one word—I could explain it: it's a *challenge*. You know what I mean. And I think I could speak for all of us. It's just a challenge. When you see a guy do a trick.

EDDIE: It's not really challenging no more. It's getting too easy now.

RALPH: We do the same trick, and we try to do it better. It's just a challenge. When we see a person do a trick, we're going to try to do it. But it's also fun at the same time.

EMILIO: It feels better. We do something else better.

RALPH: Exactly, and with style. So you doing the trick better, with style.

EDDIE: I thought he was going to say one word. That wasn't one word. That was one book!

MIKE R.: I was a baseball player, but I quit. I got into skating . . . it was more fun.

EMILIO: He quit school to skate!

MIKE R.: It was more fun.

BOTTOM'S UP
Productions

Dancers Bookings Available
For All Ocassions
orce, bachelors party, funerals, etc

FLAVA   (917) 775-9856
RO·MANCE   (917) 773-2927
RISK   (917) 782-9352

Richie and Pam at an indoor state park in Ohio

This is Pamela, My beautiful fiance. this was taken in NY on Feb 2000, we had such a great time. This party was the baby shower that we had. our baby is Due on May 31st, its exciting to know that Me little Richie will have a little Richie to look after, If he's just like me then we will have a hand ful. OHIO will be great For little Richie Johanny Velasquez, but I will show my son where I grew up in.

Right now we are at about 8 months and the Pregnancy has been an experience. We are doing great together. Of course I wish I was with my family because I miss them so Much.

...fun, exciting, & very well spent. our friendship & we grew stronger every day. We spent [a] year together in NY and then decided to go to Camp Woodward to work in the summer. This camp is the largest extreme sports camp in the world. Seeing Richie work with the kids all the dedication

* Hello, My name is Pamela Stevens and as you can see, This picture documents a very special moment for Richie & I. Almost 2 years ago, I was visiting NY City to look at graduate schools. (Im from Dayton, OH) I decided to visit a local skate park in Riverside when I met by fate... The man I'd soon start my life & future with. We soon found our selves falling more & more in Love and living together in Queens, NY. Every-day together was "Focusing on Kids".

put forth... I found myself falling even more in love with him. My undergraduate work is in psychology his love for kids inspired me. ☺ After camp, I came home to visit for a month before I headed back to the city. Richie came to visit for a week before he headed back to. 5 weeks later .... I found out I was going to have a baby and wow ... did my mind whirl. I was getting ready to start my schooling at NYU. (I was planning on getting my masters in developmental psy). I knew I didn't want to raise a baby in NYC though away from my family & twin sister. So, I made the decision to stay in ohio & raise my child. Richie again was amazing... my dream come true. He was overly excited about our baby and left his home town & family to be with his New addition soon to come. our baby is due in may and we are doing great adjusting to all the New changes. I know Richie really misses his family & friends. But he knows they are very proud of him and love him very much! We thank everyone for all there support.

Richie and Pam's wedding in Ohio

By 2000 the group was breaking up: Mike R. took a job with the Metropolitan Transit Authority; Mike M. was attending cooking school; Stephen was still working at the nail salon; Eddie moved to upstate New York and back again; Anthony was working as a subcontractor installing windows in Queens; Emilio, Jesus, and Victor had moved to Florida; and Richie was skating competitively. He and his wife, Pam, were living in Queens with their baby. Uly joined the army in 2001. The year before I had spent Thanksgiving with him. He and Dee had cooked dinner for his father, his mother and her husband, and for Dee's daughter, Nikki. And for me. I had become part of the family.

In February 2003 Uly called me from Hunter Army Airfield at Fort Stewart in Savannah, Georgia. He seemed older, more mature, and there was a sense of urgency in his voice. It was as if we were talking for the last time. I called him the next day to make plans to see him the weekend before he left for Kuwait.

What began as an interest in a group of kids trying to grow up in the Southside, relatively unscathed, with a passion for skating, grew into lasting friendships. We don't see as much of each other as we did; the "gang" has dispersed, moved away, gotten jobs, started families, gone to school. Richie, now one of the top U.S. skaters, lives in California with Pam, and their son, Johanny, managing an X-treme sports camp. Uly is still in the army, after serving in the Middle East, fighting the U.S. government's war against Iraq. Emilio stops by when he's visiting the Southside. I see Mike R., Mike M., and Mike O. occasionally on their way home from work. Eddie will call from time to time to see how things are going.

I think about when I met all the skaters who appear in this book. They were kids on the street, blading in large groups, congregating in vacant lots, neighborhood parks, sidewalks, macadam schoolyards— anywhere they could skate. They had their dreams, their plans; they had their lives ahead of them.

Uly and his mom on Thanksgiving

I told you, a month and a half ago I tried to volunteer to go 'cause I'd been wanting to go ever since
that shit happened . . . in New York. I didn't want to join the army and just be one of them [soldiers]
that been here all their lives and actually contribute nothing significant as far as going to war and what
have you. So now, you know what I'm saying, now I'm ready to go. They already told me I have to go;
I have no choice, so I have to drop everything. I'm in this new relationship, you know . . . that sucks—
before, I didn't feel the way I feel now.

   The unit I'm with right now supplies all the fuel. I maintain those vehicles—the big tankers,
the trucks—make sure that they're sending fuel to the front lines. Well, actually, they deliver fuel in bulk,
so if that fuel doesn't get delivered then our vehicles aren't movin'. So in reality, if something's gonna
get hit, and they want to hit something that's gonna put a big hurtin' on us, we will be one . . . we will
be one of the main places they will want to hit. You take out the source of energy and what do you got?
The whole army, everything works off of our fuel—the whole country does—we're going to war for
one of those reasons.

   I sit down any free time I get now, like riding over here in the car, I listen to all the songs I like.
You can take CDs and radios over there but really you can't. I'm gonna miss songs, sittin' down listening
to music—just watching TV, calling my friends up, just all that. You get a taste of it every time you go
train out in the field . . . of how it is . . . and when you go train out in the field for three days, a week,
two weeks, you're so fucking happy to be home.

   I don't have a return date as it is on my orders. I got a day of departure, but got no date to come
back. So I could be over there a year without no newspaper, nothing. The only outside contact you have is
people sending you letters. That's so important. Some people realize, but others don't know how
important one little letter is. Boy you miss that shit. I thought when I was leaving on basic training—
I told Demarys and them, don't write to me. I want to keep my head clear. But then everybody's receiving
letters. Once I got my first letter, I was addicted. I was like, man, I couldn't wait for the next day. Every
time they do a mail call, everybody's waiting there for letters.

Uly, Fort Stewart, Georgia

Demarys holding Uly's army photo

I had to do my will and all that shit. . . . It's too easy to get killed out there. I haven't thought about it much. I think maybe twice I thought about dying. But it's not like it crosses my mind and I dwell on it. I don't sit there and get depressed over it. Just God forbid . . . if it happens, I hope it happens quick [laugh].

Shit, yeah man, I fuckin' wanted to chill over here. That was my big plan believe it or not; it sounds simple as hell, but I was gonna come down here and buy me a big old fuckin' pop-up camper that has two king-sized beds. You know that was my big fucking plan right there. . . . Ah, man . . . there's so much I want to see . . . there's so much. I want to go up to freakin' Canada, just take a drive up to Canada and see Niagara Falls. All my trips have to do with just seeing shit like that. Niagara Falls.

There's a freakin' little secret that I kept that I ain't telling nobody, not my mom, my father, nobody. You know, them being my best friends and I didn't tell them, and I felt fucked up you know. I told her I wouldn't tell them. I'm gonna tell you—you know I consider you family. Before I left—before I came down here—I married Demarys. All right, the only reason I didn't tell anyone was because it wasn't for the right reasons. The only reason I married her was because—you know—because she gets her seizures and shit; she gets her seizures, and I wanted to give her medical benefits.

Richie, Johanny, and I sat down, and we were like you know what . . . and we said exactly what's going on right now, like yo . . . we'll each end up probably our own way—you know we're going to be doing our thing—we always got to keep in touch. You know we're like brothers, they're like my brothers, you know what I'm saying. I'm quick to jump on somebody for disrespecting them for the littlest shit, quicker then I would for myself. And we talked about it. We won't see each other for a while, got to keep in contact. We each gonna branch out and do our own thing—to better ourselves, and that's exactly what happened. The next time we got together was Richie's wedding. Then we were all together, you know. I'll see Richie or I'll see Johanny, or Johanny'll see Richie or see me, like that. That's how it works out, but never together. That day for the wedding we got together, we were freakin' crying, crying like babies for like a good half-hour. Just how fucked up it was, shit is working out like this. Well, we cried about it, we talked about it, and again went on our ways to do our different things you know. . . . Shit, I've always felt like the odd one 'cause shit, I didn't finish school. Johanny finished high school and was

going to college; Richie finished high school, went to college, got married, did his family;
I didn't have nothing. My situation was a lot different than theirs, and I had to understand that. When
it was time and I was ready, I got my GED and started college at LaGuardia. Then they called me up
and told me they had my shit ready to go, and I dropped all my classes and came into the army, and you
know, I don't regret nothing. I don't regret leaving school and coming over here. This is what I wanted
to do, and I just see it as a stepping-stone, you know. I'm going to get what I can out of this, and I feel
good that I did something, and am involved somehow in something—it wasn't necessarily to defend
the country—but in something. Yeah, I think we've all been like that. Yeah, I feel like I've accomplished
a lot just going through basic training. I gave up a lot. I gave up my freedom.

Well, here I am on North 11th street, doing one of the things I do best, I think this Picture was taken in the summer of 97. I was always out on my skates. I enjoyed skating very much... I still do, its not Becaus I want to create a career out of it its about being out doing something that you love. I enjoyed the thrill, the adventure, the freedom I felt when I would go to Manhattan and skate the streets from the Williamsburg Bridge to Central Park and back.

Through Out my life skating Ive met the most amazing People. from New York, to California, To Puerto Rico, to Europe. All of the friends Ive met all of the people I will miss, it is a truley Amazing adventure that I have experienced.

Zebid Sith
2000

Change defines city neighborhoods. An influx of artists (I was one of them) was followed more recently by the arrival of young urban professionals. As the Southside changes, I worry that the flavor of the community, dominated by people of Puerto Rican and Dominican descent, will disappear. New welfare regulations bring yet more changes; gentrification encroaches from every direction with its new businesses. The new prosperity and opportunities are not as accessible to Hispanic youth; many move away to pursue their goals and dreams or to raise families in safer, middle-class neighborhoods. Brooklyn at times seems a crazy quilt of ethnic and class divisions. Even in transition, the Southside remains a neighborhood on welfare. It is a tough but resilient community where human frailties and human strengths still exist side by side.

Two books that were central to my understanding of the Southside were Geoffrey Canada's *fist stick knife gun* and Jonathan Kozol's *Amazing Grace*, but it was from my own experience, documenting and living in the neighborhood, that I began to see myself as part of this community. I understand now why the bladers had no skate parks and why their attempts to build one were thwarted by the community board; why cars and streets in the Southside lay buried under banks of unplowed snow for weeks while in other neighborhoods it was removed within days; why my neighbors had such difficulty petitioning for stop signs at a dangerous intersection near P.S. 84; why I could not serve, without bias, as a juror on a local case involving injuries to a teenager because I knew about absentee landlords and egregious code violations in Southside apartment buildings. Working with Musica Against Drugs, teaching photography to former drug users, gave me more insight than any course on political and social activism could have. Simple hellos and smiles opened up communication and fostered lasting friendships to this day. The Southside became my home. I lived here during the ten years the bladers called me "their photographer" and continue to live here now.

ACKNOWLEDGMENTS

This book is dedicated to my parents, who gave me love and support and the tools to see past my own life so I could share the experiences of others and learn from them.

We Skate Hardcore developed over a period of nine years with immeasurable help and encouragement from many people. First and foremost, I wish to thank all the people of the Southside in Brooklyn, New York, and particularly the bladers for welcoming me into their lives: to Richie and Uly and their families for their continued friendship; to Anthony, Eddie, Mike R., Emilio, Mike M., Dean, Stephen, Demarys, Pam, Johanny, Juanito, Ricky, Alex, Mike O., Mecca, Michelle, Michelle M., Dennis, Adrian, Jesus, Victor, Elton, Popo, Herbz, and Shorty. Thanks also to Nelson, Maria, Sugeiry, Scarface, Mario, and their families.

I am forever indebted to the following people who were invaluable in creating this book: Iris Tillman Hill and Alexa Dilworth, my editors at the Center for Documentary Studies for their uncompromising dedication to documentary photography books; Yolanda Cuomo and Kristi Norgaard for their skill and good humor in honing the design of the book; Barbara Tannenbaum for her sincere and candid support and her eloquent essay; Jeffrey Hoone and Gary Hesse of LightWork for providing me with their insight and the opportunity of an extended artist-in-residence position when I began putting the book together in my mind, and on paper; Juan Sanchez for his poetic insight on living in the Southside; Tim Bouldry for the incredible job he did editing the video; my assistants Tony Law, for his sharp eyes and computer skills, which were essential to producing the first book design, and Hyoungsun Ha, for his ability to make my negatives sing as beautiful prints, and Einat Bar, for her help in designing my web site and DVD, and for keeping my work and life in order throughout the production of the book. I am honored and grateful.

The production of this book would not have been possible without support from the following people and institutions: Robert Byrd and the Jerome Foundation for its generous grant; the F. Lammot Belin Arts Scholarship for support in the early stages of the project; Barbara Hitchcock and the Polaroid International Collection for providing me with film and cameras throughout; Iris Tillman Hill of the Center for Documentary Studies for her initial encouragement and sound advice; Steve Maikowski, Eric Zinner, and the great staff at New York University Press for understanding the project and recognizing the validity and appropriateness of the book to the press's mission. I wish to especially thank Mary Cianni, my sister, for her relentless love and munificence throughout the years, and Joan Morgenstern for her generosity and for always coming through when needed the most. My gratitude also extends to those people who have supported the book with their thoughtful contributions: Edward Osowski, for sponsoring Barbara Tannenbaum's essay; Bill Mindlin; Bill Hunt; Robert Venuti; Patrick Keyes; Harry Kulkowitz; Keith De Lellis; Dr. Susan A. Ventre; Fred Cianni; Sarah Morthland; Anthony and Mildred Piento; Mary Ann and Peter Vilas; Stacey Tesseyman and Patsy Roth; Michael and Deborah Curry; Drs. Mary Roman and Ellen Birenbaum; Dorothy O'Beirne; Frances Cianni; Lucretia Carney; Anatole Pohorilenko; Curt LaBombard; Janet Rizzo; Romayne Cianni; Thomas and Elizabeth O'Rourke; Todd Fleidner; Heidi Czarny; Vicki Harris; Alison Nordstrom; Laurence Miller; and Brian Paul Clamp.

My appreciation and gratitude also extends to the people whose friendship as well as intellectual and conceptual guidance helped channel my ideas and energies to see this project through: Susan Lipper, Anatole Pohorilenko, and Edward Osowski; Daile Kaplan, Jonathan Anderson, Edwin Hock Low, Linda Ferrer, and David B. Waller. And to those people and institutions whose generous support and trust in my work grace these pages from front to back: Alison Nordstrom (Southeast Museum of Photography), Anne Sanciaud (Bibliothèque Nationale de France), Roy Flukinger (Harry Ransom Humanities Research Center), Bob Shamis (The Museum of the City of New York), Richard B. Woodward (*DoubleTake*), Elizabeth Smith (The Photographers' Gallery, London), Neil Trager (The Samuel Dorsky Museum), Juan Alberto Gaviria (Centro Colombo Americano), Barbara Millstein (The Brooklyn Museum), Anne Wilkes Tucker (The Museum of Fine Arts, Houston), Thierry Martin, Finn Thrane (Museet for Fotokunst), David Acton (Worcester Art Museum), Jill DeVonyear and Marianne Frisch (The Reader's Digest Collection), Brooklyn Union Gas, Musée Pierre Noël, Catherine Ware, Dennis Grousosky, Gina Ruef, Claude Bos, and Hans Sowa. I thank you.

I am grateful to those people who have given me the opportunity to share ideas with them and my work with others: Daniel Bargallo, David Brittain, Phillip Brookman, Stephen Bulger, Julie Burke, Jean Caslin, Harris Fogel, Vance Gellert, Howard Greenberg, Tina Hay, Elizabeth Levine, James Luciano, Stephen Mayes, Anne MacDonald, Thomas McGovern, Kerri Pickett, Orville Robertson, Mark Sealy, George Slade, Mary Virginia Swanson, Helena Tovar, Alma Villegas, Wendy Watriss, and Jonathan Ziegler.

I am forever indebted to my family and friends—you know who you are; to Stacey, Bessie, and Chardelle for their spiritual guidance; to Nancy and Stefan for exploring the Southside with me; to Jesse for his pictures; to Matthew for being there at key times; and to the students I've taught at Parsons School of Design, you keep me thinking and looking.

In memory of my father, Scott, Michael, and Jonathan.

New York University Press
Washington Square
New York, NY 10003
www.nyupress.org

Lyndhurst Books
Center for Documentary Studies at Duke University
http://cds.aas.duke.edu

The handwritten texts are by the in-line skaters of the Southside, Brooklyn, New York.
All photographs are by Vincent Cianni, except for those on pages 41 (Michelle),
46, and 64 by Richie Velasquez; pages 65, 125–26, 149, and 152–53 by Mike Ruiz; pages 82–83
by Eddie Miejas; and pages 58–59 and 130–31 by various photographers (including author).

This book was made possible by a grant from the Jerome Foundation.

Lyndhurst Books, the imprint of the Center for Documentary Studies,
are published with support from the Lyndhurst Foundation.

Library of Congress Cataloging-in-Publication Data
Cianni, Vincent.
We Skate Hardcore : photographs from Brooklyn's Southside / Vincent Cianni.
p. cm.
ISBN 0-8147-1642-3 (cloth : alk. paper)
1. In-line skating—New York (State)—New York.
2. In-line skating—New York (State)—New York—Pictorial works.
3. Brooklyn (N.Y.)
4. Brooklyn (N.Y.)—Pictorial works.   I. Title.

GV859.73.C55 2004
796.21'09747'1—dc22   2004042616

Designed by Yolanda Cuomo and Vincent Cianni
Design associate, Kristi Norgaard

Printed and bound in China

10 9 8 7 6 5 4 3 2 1